INVENTORS BY MISTAKE

by
Rebecca Phillips-Bartlett

Minneapolis, Minnesota

Credits

All images are courtesy of Shutterstock.com, unless otherwise specified. With thanks to Getty Images, Thinkstock Photo, and iStockphoto.

Recurring images – Andrew Rybalko, cosmaa, davooda, P-fotography, Mark Rademaker. Cover – davooda, Andrew Rybalko, dimair, cosmaa, P-fotography. 2–3 – Nastya Trel, Cofefe. 4–5 – Sharomka. 6–7 – Materialscientist, Top Vector Studio, Tatahnka, Yeti studio. 8–9 – Net Vector, LuYago, Lilanakani, Siberian Art, Materialscientist. 10–11 – Kateryna Kon, Ducksoup. 12–13 – ApoGapo, Prostorina, Cofefe, ZOVICOTA. 14–15 – Bettmann, robuart, Andrei Kuzmik, Svetlana_Smirnova. 16–17 – INTERFOTO, Biscotto Design, Nastya Trel, AlenKadr. 18–19 – Wikimedia Commons/Public Domain, Dzm1try, Lyudmyla Kharlamova. 20–21 – Stocksnapper, Ekaterina_Minaeva, futuristman, Vladimir Konstantinov. 22–23 – Narint Asawaphisith, stockpexel.

Library of Congress Cataloging-in-Publication Data

Names: Phillips-Bartlett, Rebecca, 1999- author.
Title: Inventors by mistake / by Rebecca Phillips-Bartlett.
Description: Minneapolis, Minnesota : Bearport Publishing Company, [2024] | Series: Brilliant people, big ideas | Includes index.
Identifiers: LCCN 2023030958 (print) | LCCN 2023030959 (ebook) | ISBN 9798889163572 (library binding) | ISBN 9798889163626 (paperback) | ISBN 9798889163664 (ebook)
Subjects: LCSH: Inventions--Juvenile literature. | Inventors--Juvenile literature.
Classification: LCC T48 .P49 2024 (print) | LCC T48 (ebook) | DDC 609.2--dc23/eng/20230711
LC record available at https://lccn.loc.gov/2023030958
LC ebook record available at https://lccn.loc.gov/2023030959

© 2024 BookLife Publishing
This edition is published by arrangement with BookLife Publishing.

North American adaptations © 2024 Bearport Publishing Company. All rights reserved. No part of this publication may be reproduced in whole or in part, stored in any retrieval system, or transmitted in any form or by any means, electronic, mechanical, photocopying, recording, or otherwise, without written permission from the publisher.

For more information, write to Bearport Publishing, 5357 Penn Avenue South, Minneapolis, MN 55419.

Contents

Big Ideas 4
George Crum and Catherine Adkins Wicks ... 6
Wilhelm Conrad Röntgen 8
Alexander Fleming 10
Percy Spencer 12
Frank Epperson 14
Ruth Graves Wakefield 16
Dr. Spencer Silver and Arthur Fry 18
The Hall of Fame 20
All You Need Is an Idea! 22
Glossary 24
Index 24

Big Ideas

Think of all the amazing **inventions** we use every day. Did you know some of them started as big mistakes?

From chocolate chip cookies to sticky notes, who do we have to thank for these amazing inventions? Meet the chefs, scientists, and inventors who turned big mistakes into **brilliant** ideas.

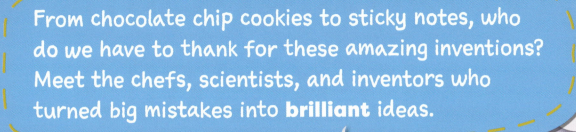

Let's find out which mistakes turned into amazing inventions!

George Crum and Catherine Adkins Wicks

"One of us **accidentally** invented potato chips."

"But no one can remember who it was...."

1824–1914

AROUND 1815–1917

Potato Chips

Some people think George Crum invented potato chips. George was a chef, and his customers wanted thinner fries. So, he cut the potatoes into little slices and **fried** them until they were crisp.

What is your favorite flavor of potato chips?

Other people think George's sister, Catherine Adkins Wicks, was the real inventor. They think she made the first chips when she accidentally dropped a thin slice of potato into the fryer.

Wilhelm Conrad Röntgen

"When I was working in my lab, I noticed something odd!"

1845–1923

X-Rays

Alexander Fleming

While working in the lab, I found something growing!

1881–1955

Penicillin

Alexander Fleming was doing an **experiment** with dishes of **bacteria**. He left the dishes on the lab table and went away. When he came back, the dishes had **mold**.

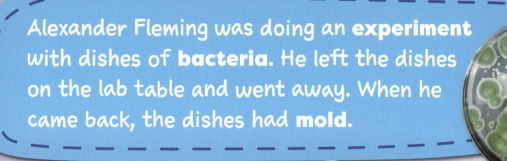

Alexander noticed that the bacteria around the mold was dying. He used this mold to make a medicine called penicillin (*pen-i-SIL-uhn*).

Penicillin helps people fight germs.

Percy Spencer

I made a mistake that can cook tasty meals!

1894–1970

Microwave Oven

Percy Spencer was an **engineer**. One day, he was working on a machine that sent out energy. As he stood nearby, the candy bar in his pocket melted.

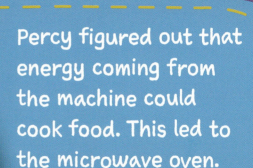

Percy figured out that energy coming from the machine could cook food. This led to the microwave oven.

Percy placed popcorn seeds near the machine and they popped!

Frank Epperson

"I was 11 years old when I invented frozen treats!"

1894–1983

Frozen Treats

One day, Frank Epperson used a stick to mix himself a drink in a cup. He left his sweet drink outside at the end of the day. He forgot it for the whole night.

It got so cold at night that the drink froze on the mixing stick. The next day, Frank ate his drink off the stick. This was the first frozen treat!

What is your favorite frozen treat on a stick?

Ruth Graves Wakefield

I love chocolate cookies! Let me try something new....

1903–1977

Chocolate Chip Cookies

Ruth Graves Wakefield accidentally invented chocolate chip cookies. Ruth was trying to make chocolate cookies. She put chocolate pieces in the **dough** thinking they would melt.

Have you ever made chocolate chip cookies?

But instead of melting, the chocolate pieces stayed together. Ruth had made cookies with chocolate chunks inside!

Dr. Spencer Silver and Arthur Fry

"We are both scientists."

1941–2021

"We worked together to invent sticky notes!"

1931–now

Sticky Notes

18

Dr. Spencer Silver wanted to make a stronger glue. But what he ended up with was not very sticky or strong.

Meanwhile, Arthur Fry's bookmarks kept falling out. He thought Spencer's glue could keep them in place and let them be easily moved whenever he wanted. Together, Spencer and Arthur invented sticky notes.

The Hall of Fame

Here are some other brilliant unplanned inventions that deserve a place in our Hall of Fame.

Ice Cream Cones

There are many stories about who invented ice cream cones. One story says that an ice cream seller ran out of bowls, so he started selling ice cream in waffles rolled into cones.

Hook and Loop

George de Mestral studied burrs to find out what made them stick. He invented hook and loop **fastenings** based on these plants!

A burr

Modeling Clay

Did you know that modeling clay was first invented for cleaning? Later, people realized it was a fun toy, too!

All You Need Is an Idea!

From X-rays to frozen treats, many amazing inventions wouldn't be around without these brilliant people.

They turned big mistakes into brilliant inventions. All you need is one idea to lead to lots of amazing things!

What could you try to invent?

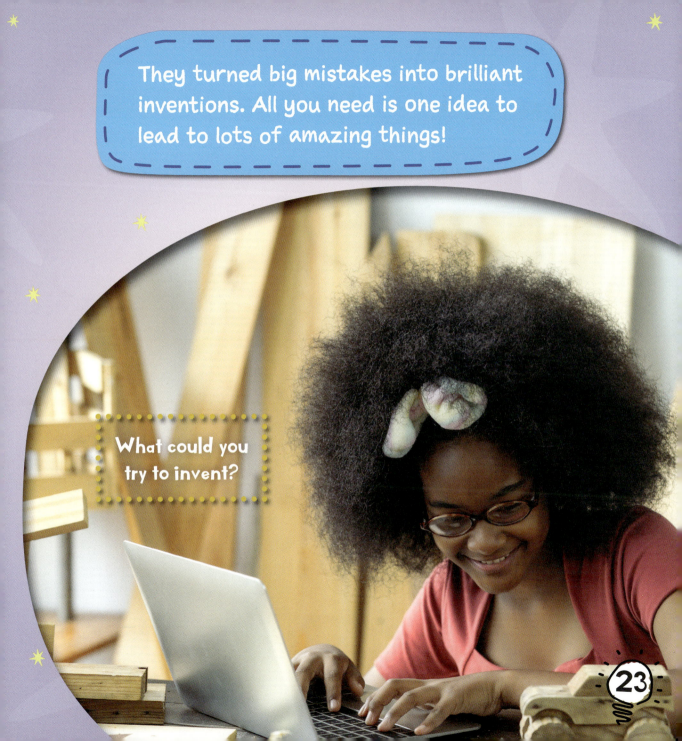

23

Glossary

accidentally happening by mistake

bacteria tiny living things that can make people sick

brilliant extremely smart

dough a sticky, thick mixture that is used to make cookies

engineer a person who designs or builds things

experiment a scientific test

fastenings things that attach or join things together

fried cooked in hot oil

inventions new things that have been made to solve problems

mold a living thing that grows on damp surfaces

Index

chefs 5, 7
chocolate 5, 13, 16–17
frozen treats 14–15, 22
ice cream 20
microwave 12–13

penicillin 10–11
potato chips 6–7
scientists 5, 9, 18
sticky notes 5, 18–19
X-rays 8–9, 22